CW00722920

Published 2002

Editor: Chris Harvey
Cover Design: Space DPS Limited

International MUSIC Publications

© International Music Publications Limited
Griffin House 161 Hammersmith Road London W6 8BS England

Boom

words and music by
Anastacia Newkirk and Glenn Ballard

highest chart position not available at time of publication

release date 10th June 2002

did you know Anastacia has two prominent tattoos – the first, on her back, is an Ankh surrounded by an Egyptian sun representing 'eternal life'. The second tat is between her shoulder-blades and stands for 'forever' or 'permanence'

Bop Bop Baby

words and music by
**Chris O'Brien, Graham Murphy,
Brian McFadden and Shane Filan**

highest chart position 5
release date 20th May 2002

did you know Westlife's celebrity "engagements" include Bryan McFadden and former Atomic Kitten star Kerry Katona and Nicky Byrne and Georgina Ahern, the daughter of recently re-elected Irish Taoiseach Bertie Ahern

1. My mum al-ways said___ no-thing would break___ me___ or lead me a-stray.___

Verse 2:
On a love train. twenty odd years now
I got off today
But nobody said the stop that I've taken
Was a stop too late
Now I'm alone I'm thinking of stupid
Hurtful small things like,

When I call you at home *etc.*

Corner Of The Earth

words and music by
Jason Kay and Robert Harris

highest chart position Outside Top 75

release date 24th June 2002

did you know Jay Kay bought his current 70-acre Buckinghamshire spread for a cool £1.4 million in 1998, meaning he's got plenty of garage space for his fleet of vintage Ferraris. It also has two trout-filled lakes, mini-waterfalls, organic vegetables and geese

La la la la. La la la

la. La la la la.

D.%. al Coda
Play 4 times ad lib.

Coda

it smiles at me.

Repeat ad lib. to fade

DJ

words and music by
Graham Stack and Paul Rein

highest chart position 3
release date 6th May 2002

did you know H & Claire are a duo drawn from the ashes of teen pop sensation Steps. After the band's demise they were both offered recording contracts but, as they confessed, "we were just too chicken to do it on our own!"

Don't Let Me Get Me

highest chart position 6
release date 13th May 2002
did you know Another single from her mega-successful *Missundaztood* album, this track features a themed video which follows Pink back to her high school, before she's promised pop stardom in exchange for "changing everything you are'

words and music by
Alecia Moore and Dallas Austin

Moderately

Nev - er ___ win first place, ___ I don't sup - port the team, ___ I can't take di - rec - tion and my

L. A. told me, ___ you'll be a pop star, ___ all you have ___ to change is

Instrumental solo

socks are nev - er ___ clean. Teach - ers dat - ed me, ___ my ___ par - ents hat - ed me, ___

ev - 'ry - thing you ___ are. Tired of being com - pared ___ to ___ damn Brit - ney Spears,

To Coda

I was al - ways in a fight, ___ 'cause I can't do noth - ing right. ___

she's so pret - ty, ___ that's ___ just ain't me. ___

Dreamer

words and music by
**Marti Frederiksen, Ozzy Osbourne
and Michael Jones**

highest chart position 18
release date 3rd June 2002

did you know The former Black Sabbath singer and bat-devouring Brum has become an unlikely soap stars via the MTV series *The Osbournes*, attracting record audiences as its hero struggles to come to terms with everyday domestic problems

1. Gaz-ing through the win-dow at the world out-side,
won-der-ing will Mo-ther Earth sur-vive,
hop-ing that man-kind will stop a-bus-
-ing her some-time.

yeah.

Guitar

D.%. al Coda

4. If

Coda

I'm just a dream - er___ who's search - ing for___ the way___

Verse 4:
If only we could all just find serenity
It would be nice if we all could live as one
When will all this anger, hate and bigotry
Be gone?

I'm just a dreamer *etc.*

Escape

words and music by

Enrique Iglesias, Kara Dio Guardi, Steve Morales and David Siegel

highest chart position 3
release date 13th May 2002
did you know Enrique initially found it difficult to step out from the shadow of his father's huge legacy. Indeed, several majors rejected his efforts before he finally broke through with his 1995 debut album. His career trajectory was temporarily impeded by his reluctance to embrace English-language recordings

Everything

words and music by
Marion Ravn, Marit Larsen,
Peter Zizzo and Jimmy Bralower

highest chart position not available at time of publication

release date not known at time of publication

did you know M2M are Marit and Marion, who met when they were five years old. They developed a penchant for duets, while acting in musicals. Their first record deal, in 1994, resulted in an album of songs for Norwegian children, which won a nomination for a Norwegian Grammy

Freak Like Me

highest chart position 1
release date 22nd April 2002

did you know The Sugababes are a trio of Keisha, Mutya and Heidi. Heidi is the newest member, who was in the original formation of Atomic Kitten in her native Liverpool, while Keisha and Mutya had been signed to a record deal aged only 14 before they hit with the single 'Overload'

words and music by

Gary Numan, Eugene Hanes, Marc Valentine, Loren Hill, William Collins, George Clinton and Gary Cooper

1. Let me lay it on the line, I got-ta lit-tle

(Verse 2 see block lyrics)

frea-ki-ness in-side. And you know that a man has got-ta deal

Verse 2:
Boy you're moving kind of slow
You gotta keep it up now there you go
That's just one thing that a man must do
I'm packing all the flavours you need
I got you shook up on your knees
'Cause it's all about the dog in me.

I wanna freak in the morning *etc.*

Full Moon

words and music by
Michael Flowers

highest chart position 15
release date 17th June 2002

did you know After making a huge impact with her self-titled debut album in 1994, Brandy Norwood chose to return to acting instead of recording a follow-up, appearing in the sitcom *Moesha* and taking the title role in Disney's 1997 made for TV movie *Cinderella*

1. Boy, I saw you soon as you came bounc-ing through the door,
2. Why is this the first time that I'm see-ing you a-round,

Girlfriend

words and music by
**Chad Hugo, Pharrell Williams
and Justin Timberlake**

highest chart position 2
release date 15th April 2002

did you know Singers Justin Timberlake and J.C. Chasez once co-starred in the Disney Channel's *The Mickey Mouse Club*. Their success in the late 90s with singles like 'I Want You Back' and 'Tearing Up My Heart' was built on a tour of roller rinks

1. I____ don't know why__ you care,
2. Does__ he know what__ you feel?

he____ does-n't e - ven know__ you're there.
Are____ you____ sure____ that____ it's real?

Bridge:

Gold

words and music by
Beverley Knight

highest chart position 27
release date 24th June 2002

did you know The fast-rising star of Brit-soul has cashed in by making herself a friend of the stars, the good and the great. She's met Nelson Mandela, and even sung happy birthday to Mohammed Ali, as well as duetting with Jamiroquai's Jay Kay

Ah,———— ah,—— ah.———

1. Some peo-ple nev-er rec-og-nise———— it,———— though it's right be-fore their eyes———— and shines in all its glo-ry, they nev-er ev-er see.

2. Gold lies in riv-ers un-dis-cov--ered,—— hid-den from the sight of those———— who don't know what to look—— for, they ain't nev-er gon-na find it.

God Save The Queen

words and music by
**Paul Cook, Glen Matlock,
Steve Jones and John Lydon**

highest chart position **15**
release date **27th May 2002**

did you know Part of the controversy surrounding the Sex Pistols' decision to reissue this during the Queen's Golden Jubilee concerned Lydon's appearance on *Richard and Judy*, where he made some surprisingly ambivalent remarks regarding the monarchy. Rebuked by such as Billy Bragg for his counter-revolutionary statements, he toughened this stance, acknowledging that the royal family "haven't being doing too well recently..."

1. God   save the Queen,   the fas - cist re - gime.
2. God   save the Queen,   she ain't no human   being.
(Verses 3-7 see block lyric)

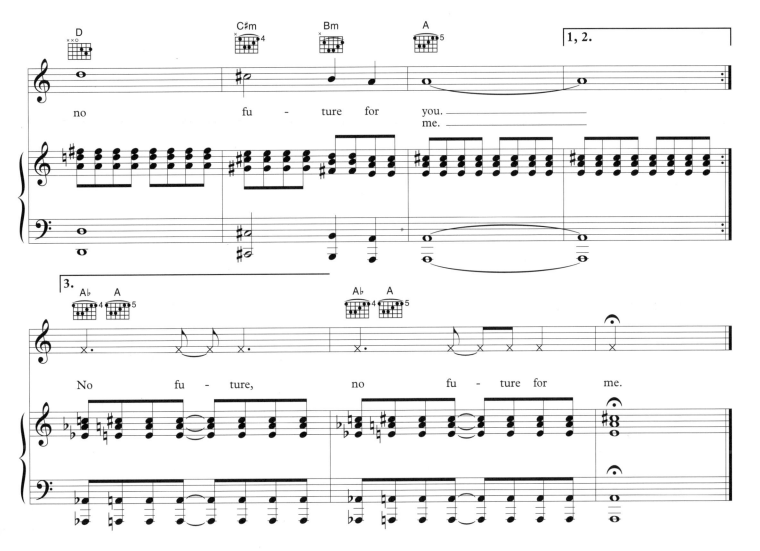

Verse 3:
God save the Queen
We mean it man
We love our Queen
God saves.

Verse 4:
God save the Queen
'Cause tourists are money
And our figurehead
Is not what she seems.

Verse 5:
Oh God save History
God save your mad parade
Lord God have mercy
All crimes are paid.

Verse 6:
God save the Queen
We mean it man
We love our Queen
God saves.

Verse 7:
God save the Queen
We mean it man
And there's no future
In England's dreaming.

How You Remind Me

words and music by

**Chad Kroeger, Michael Kroeger, Ryan Peake
and Ryan Vikedal**

highest chart position 4
release date 11th February 2002

did you know Nickelback started life as a cover band in Calgary, before singer Chad Kroeger borrowed $4,000 from his stepfather and moved to Vancouver to cut some demos. While waiting for his break he spent two years selling advertising space for a football magazine. He used his PR knowledge to get his friends to fax radio stations to help get airplay for Nickelback's first single

Drop D tuning:
⑥ = D

Moderately slow ♩ = 86

Verse:

1. Nev - er made it as a wise man,
   I could-n't cut it as a poor man steal - in'.
2. *See additional lyrics*

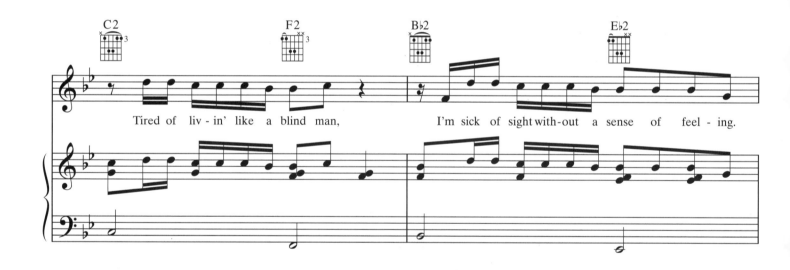

Tired of liv - in' like a blind man, I'm sick of sight with-out a sense of feel - ing.

Omit 2nd time

And this is how__ you re - mind__ me. This is how__ you re - mind__

Chorus:

D.S. % al Coda

Verse 2:
It's not like you didn't know that.
I said I love you and swear I still do.
And it must have been so bad.
'Cause livin' with me must have damn near killed you.
This is how you remind me of what I really am.
This is how you remind me of what I really am.
(To Chorus:)

It's OK

words and music by
Mikkel Eriksen, Hallgeir Rustan and Tor Erik Hermansen

highest chart position 4
release date 11th February 2002

did you know The mastermind behind Atomic Kitten's songwriting is, bizarrely enough, Andy McCluskey of fellow Liverpudlians Orchestral Manoeuvres In The Dark. It was he who founded the band in 1999 alongside Kerry Katona, Liz McLarnon and Natasha Hamilton, before Katona left the band due to her dislike of travelling

1. Well I re - mem-ber all the nights I used to stay at home,
(2.) got to where you want-ed like I knew you would,

on the phone, all night long. Used to talk a - bout the things we real - ly want to do.
cash, car, house, it's all good. Is that why you nev - er come a - round here no more

Just A Little

words and music by
**Michelle Escoffery, John Hammond-Hagan
and George Hammond-Hagan**

highest chart position 1
release date 13th May 2002
did you know Liberty X are Michelle, Jessica, Kelli, Kevin and Tony – the "other" five finalists from TV's *Pop Stars*. They were originally titled Liberty until an American band of the same name complained

Light My Fire

words and music by

**Jim Morrison, John Densmore, Robert Krieger
and Raymond Manzarek**

highest chart position 1
release date 27th May 2002

did you know Housewives' favourite and *Pop Idol* winner Will
Young once enrolled on a politics course at Exeter University –
which might account for that Tony Blair smile – before his 'calling'
kicked in. He subsequently studied musical theatre at the Arts
Educational School in Chiswick

With a beat

3rd verse only cue notes

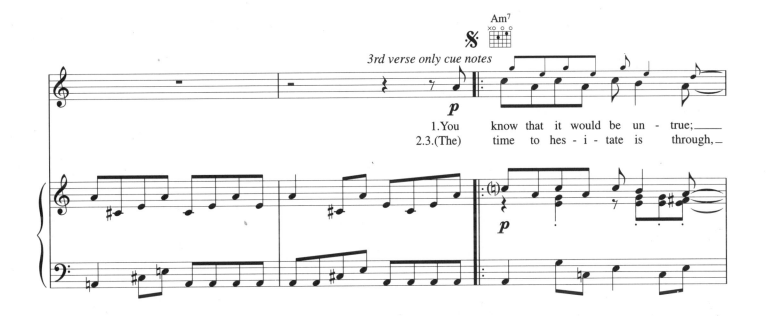

1. You know that it would be un - true;_____
2.3.(The) time to hes - i - tate is through,_____

You know that I would be a liar;_____
No time to wal - low in the mire,_____

Coda

Repeat three times

Try to set the night on fire,

Try to set the night on fire.

Kiss Kiss

words and music by
**Juliette Jaimes, Steve Welton-Jaimes
and Sezen Aksu**

highest chart position 1
release date 29th April 2002

did you know In January 2000 Holly Valance, a.k.a. Felicity Scully from *Neighbours*, made her first appearance on UK TV. Soon she had the matching pop career as she sought to emulate Kylie Minogue as Aussie girl next door-cum-Antipodean sex symbol

Mm!

Mm!

1. When you look at me, tell me what you see. This is what you get, it's the way I am.
(Verse 2 see block lyric)

Verse 2:
You could be mine baby, what's your star sign
Won't you take a step into the lions den
I can hear my conscience calling me, calling me
Say I'm gonna be a bad girl again
Why don't you come on over, we can't leave this all undone
Got a devil on my shoulder, there's no place for you to run.

You don't have to act *etc.*

Love At First Sight

highest chart position 2
release date 10th June 2002

did you know Kylie has come a long way since 'I Should Be So Lucky' – her most left-field moment to date came when she sang a duet with noted weirdo Nick Cave, 'Where The Wild Flowers Grow'. It featured Minogue, nude, floating dead in the water in the accompanying video

words and music by

Kylie Minogue, Richard Stannard, Julian Gallagher, Ashley Howes and Martin Harrington

1. Thought that I was go-ing cra-zy,— just hav-ing one of those days,– yeah;
(Verse 2 see block lyric)

did-n't know what to do,— then there was you.————— And

Verse 2:
Was tired of running out of luck
Thinking 'bout giving up, yeah
Didn't know what to do
Then there was you.

And everything went from wrong to right *etc.*

My Culture

words and music by

**Jamie Catto, Maxwell Fraser, Robert Williams,
Duncan Bridgeman, Nigel Butler and Iain MacLeod**

highest chart position 9
release date 8th April 2002
did you know 1 Giant Leap features Faithless founder Jamie Catto and producer Duncan Bridgeman, who created 'My Culture' by travelling internationally with a video camera and a laptop to capture all the marvellous sounds they encountered. The finished album sourced material from Senegal, South Africa, Uganda, Thailand, India, Australia and the UK and US

1. When I look back— ov-er the years, at the things that brought tears to my eyes, Pa-pa said we have to be wise to live long— lives. Now I re-cog-nise what my fa-ther said be-fore he died, vo-cal-ize things I've left un-said.

2. 3. This is what my Dad-dy told— me I wished he would hold me a lit-tle more than he did, but he taught me my cul-ture and how to live po-si-tive I nev-er wan-na shame the blood in my veins

Never Tear Us Apart

words and music by
Andrew Farriss and Michael Hutchence

highest chart position Outside Top 75

release date 20th May 2002

did you know Joe Cocker first topped the UK charts in November 1968 with a version of the Beatles' 'With A Little Help From My Friends'. Later he also topped the US charts with 'Up Where We Belong', his duet with Jennifer Warnes. More recently he appeared at the Queen's Golden Jubilee celebrations

Words and Music by
Andrew Farriss and Michael Hutchence

Soak Up The Sun

words and music by
Sheryl Crow and Jeff Trott

highest chart position 16
release date 1st April 2002

did you know Crow is one of the most celebrated of a new generation of American singer-songwriters, counting Keith Richards of the Rolling Stones, the Dixie Chicks, Chrissie Hynde and Eric Clapton among her fans. Indeed, all of those artists were guests on her *Live In Central Park* album of 1999

Moderately fast ♩ = 120

Verses 1&2:

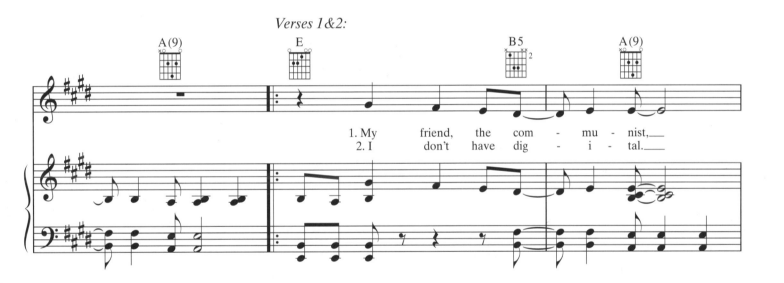

1. My friend, the com - mu - nist,___
2. I don't have dig - i - tal.___

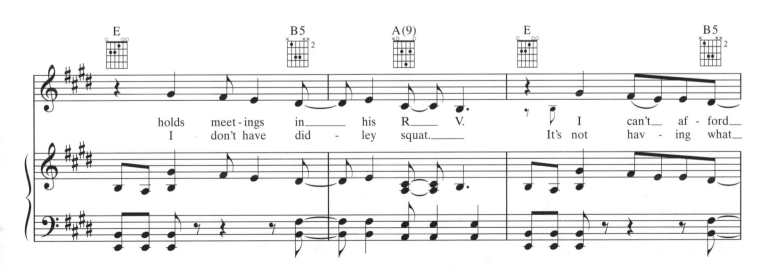

holds meet - ings in___ his R - V.
I don't have did - ley squat.___ It's not hav - ing what___
I can't___ af - ford___

114

No More Drama

highest chart position 9
release date 29th April 2002

did you know Mary J Blige first shot to fame when she sang Anita Baker's 'Caught Up In The Rapture' into a karaoke machine at a mall in White Plains. Her stepfather passed the tape on to Andre Harrell of Uptown Records, and his 'lieutenant', Sean 'Puffy' Combs, took her under his production wing, resulting in the worldwide success of her *What's The 411?* debut album

words and music by
**Terry Lewis, James Harris III,
Barry De Vorzon and Perry Botkin**

Oops (Oh My)

words and music by

Timothy Mosley, Melissa Elliott and Charlene Keys

highest chart position 5
release date 29th April 2002

did you know Tweet is a protégé of Missy 'Misdemeanor' Elliott and production whizzkid Timbaland. Prior to the overnight success of 'Oops (Oh My)', Tweet had appeared on Elliott's 'Take Away' as well as a track by new Def Jam mega-seller Ja Rule

Fast groove ♩ = 160

Verse:

1. Tell you what I did last night. I came home,__ say__
2. *See additional lyrics*

Verse 2:
I tried and I tried to avoid,
But this thing was happening.
Swallowed my pride, let it ride,
And partied.
But this body felt just like mines.
I got worried.
I looked over to my left,
A reflection of myself.
That's why I couldn't catch my breath.
(To Chorus:)

Rock The Boat

words and music by
Rapture Stewart, Eric Seats and Stephen Garrett

highest chart position 12
release date 6th May 2002

did you know As well as a burgeoning career as a singer,
by the time of her unfortunate demise photogenic R&B
prodigy Aaliyah was also starting to win recognition for
her acting roles – starring in *Romeo Must Die* while also
signing on to projected sequels to *The Matrix*

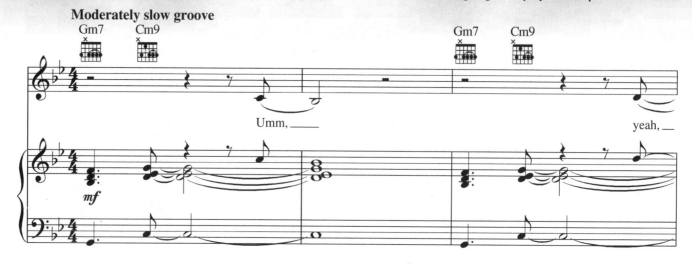

Umm, _____ yeah, _____

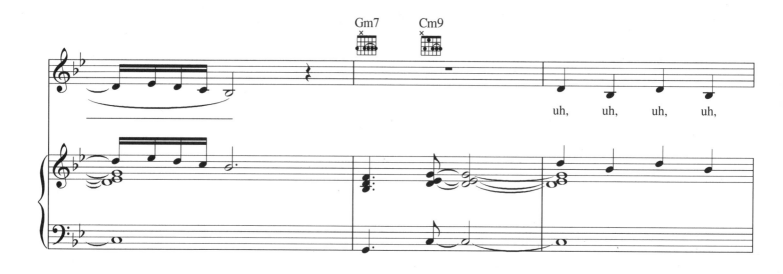

uh, uh, uh, uh,

umm___ umm, umm,_ yeah! _____ Boy you know you make me

Someone Like You

words and music by

Alistair Gordon, Gary Mahoney and Russell Watson

highest chart position 10
release date 6th May 2002

did you know Russell Watson is the most feted of recent British tenors, though he only graduated to classical music after singing in clubs around Manchester, where he was cajoled into attempting Puccini's 'Nessun Dorma'. Faye Tozer, meanwhile, is better known as 'Smiley Steps' due to her happy-go-lucky demeanour in that well loved boy/girl band

Russell

Il tem-po pas - sa sen - za che,— lo pas-so mai in-sieme a te.—

Ma ti pen-sa-vo sem-pre, nei so-gni tu— con me.— Per me il mon-do fi - ni-ra,— se

non ci fos-si tu.—— O-vun-que vai, vog-lio che sai.—— *(Faye)* 1. If you

Something To Talk About

words and music by
Damon Gough

highest chart position 28
release date 10th June 2002

did you know Badly Drawn Boy (a.k.a. Damon Gough) began recording music after meeting Andy Votel in Manchester and setting up the Twisted Nerve label together. But he came to renown first by appearing on the U.N.K.L.E. album *Psyence Fiction*, alongside such luminaries as Thom Yorke of Radiohead, and Richard Ashcroft of the Verve

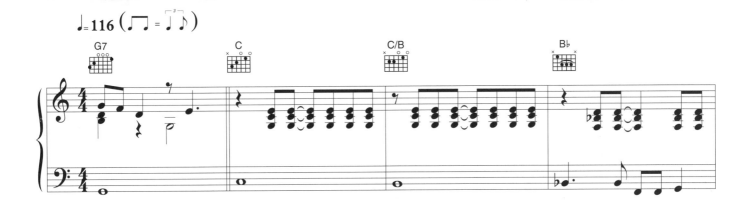

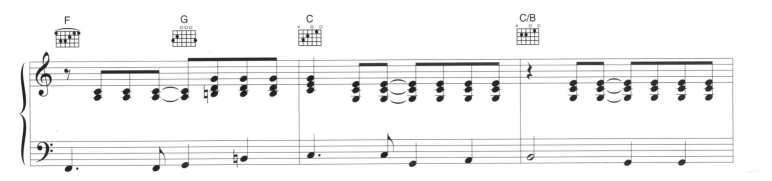

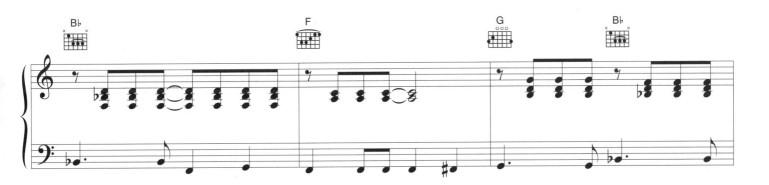

Verse 3:
I've been dreaming
Of the things I learned about a boy
Who's leaving nothing else to chance again
You've got to let me in
Or let me out.

Ooh, something to talk about *etc.*

Starbucks

words and music by

**Adam Perry, Giles Perry, Mark Chapman,
Daniel Carter and Jason Perry**

highest chart position **20**
release date **13th May 2002**

did you know **So why write a song about the coffee emporium?
Over to Dan Carter. "We had a big discussion about what we'd do
if this all ended now, and we were like, we could probably sort
something out in the long term, but we'd probably all end up
working in McDonald's. And this ridiculous conversation started,
'I'd rather work in Burger King', 'No, McDonald's is better than that.'
And it ended up with the ultimate job out of those sort of fast food
jobs would be working in Starbucks!"**

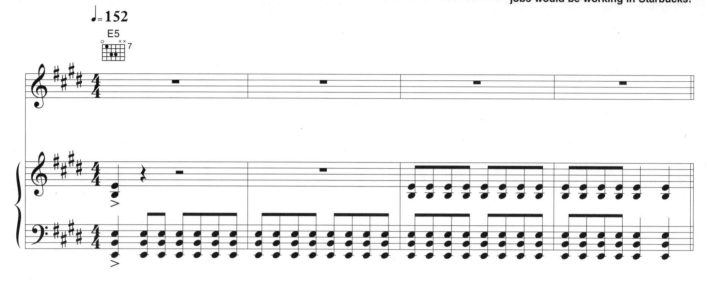

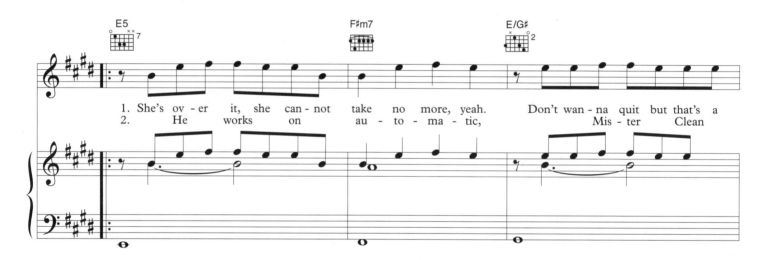

1. She's ov - er it, she can - not take no more, yeah. Don't wan - na quit but that's a
2. He works on au - to - ma - tic, Mis - ter Clean

pret - ty nice door, yeah. I got a bed it real - ly cost a for - tune,
but I doubt it. He's got to have his say,

156

There Goes My Heart Again

words and music by
Gordon Haskell

highest chart position Outside Top 75
release date 1st April 2002
did you know Before his musical career capsized and then miraculously refloated itself, Haskell's previous claim to fame came as singer for King Crimson – although he never played a live date with Robert Fripp's band, despite appearing on their *Lizard* album

And I don't know where I'm go-ing now,
And I don't think I'll be hang-ing round,
And I don't know where I'm go-ing now,

where to start or ev-en how.
some-thing inside just hit the ground.
where to start or ev-en how.

But if you see her, say hel - lo from me,

though I don't know where I am gon-na be.

I'm kind of los - ing my i - den - ti - ty,

she was the great - er part of me.

D.%. al Coda
To Coda ⊕

We Are All Made Of Stars

words and music by

Moby

highest chart position 11

release date 29th April 2002

did you know Richard Melville Hall earned his childhood nickname of Moby because the author of the great seafaring novel *Moby Dick* was his great-great grand-uncle. But before he became a dance music auteur, he cut his teeth with the Connecticut punk vandals the Vatican Commandos, as well as San Francisco's unhinged art terrorists Flipper

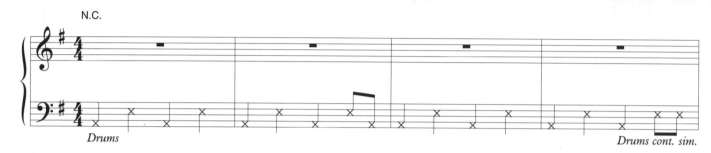

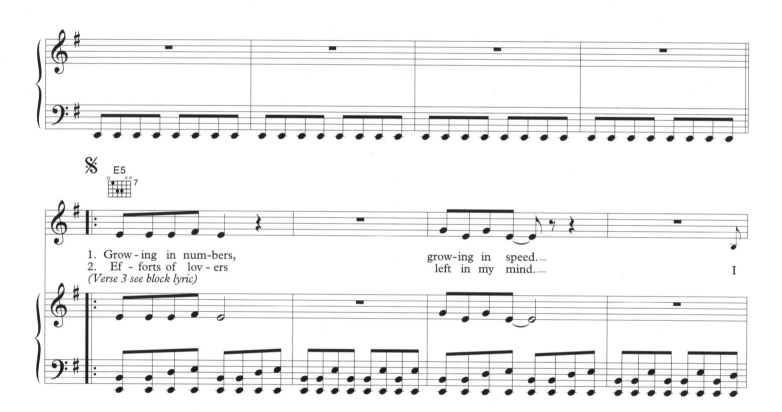

1. Grow-ing in num-bers, grow-ing in speed.—
2. Ef - forts of lov - ers left in my mind.—
(Verse 3 see block lyric)

Can't fight the fu - ture, can't fight what I see.—
sing in the reach-es we'll see what we find.—

Verse 3:
Slowly rebuilding,
I feel it in me.
Growing in numbers,
And growing in peace.

People, they come together *etc.*

Karaoke Classics
9696A   PVG/CD   ISBN: 1-84328-202-X

Back For Good - Delilah - Hey Baby - I Will Always Love You - I Will Survive - Let Me Entertain You - Reach - New York, New York - Summer Nights - Wild Thing

Party Hits
9499A   PVG/CD   ISBN: 1-84328-097-8

Come On Eileen - Dancing Queen - Groove Is In The Heart - Hi Ho Silver Lining - Holiday - House Of Fun - The Loco-Motion - Love Shack - Staying Alive - Walking On Sunshine

Disco
9493A   PVG/CD   ISBN: 1-84328-091-4

I Feel Love - I Will Survive - I'm So Excited - Lady Marmalade - Le Freak - Never Can Say Goodbye - On The Radio - Relight My - Fire - YMCA - You Sexy Thing

School Disco
9709A   PVG/CD   ISBN: 1-84328-212-7

Baggy Trousers – Club Tropicana – December 1963 (Oh What A Night) – The Final Countdown – Karma Chameleon – The One And Only – Material Girl – Relax – Stand And Deliver – Take On Me

all woman

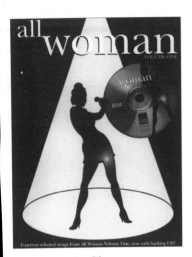

**ALL WOMAN
VOLUME 1 PVG/CD 7077A**

All Woman - Cabaret - Can't Stay Away
From You - Eternal Flame - Ev'ry Time We
Say Goodbye - Get Here - I Am What I Am
I Only Want To Be With You - Miss You
Like Crazy - Nobody Does It Better
The Rose - Summertime - Superwoman
What's Love Got To Do With It

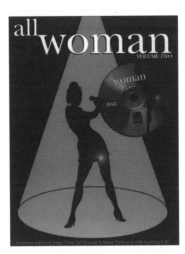

**ALL WOMAN
VOLUME 2 PVG/CD 7268A**

Anytime You Need A Friend
Don't It Make My Brown Eyes Blue
Flashdance....What A Feeling - I'll Stand
By You - Killing Me Softly With His Song
One Moment In Time - Pearl's A Singer
(They Long To Be) Close To You - Think
True Blue - Walk On By - The Wind
Beneath My Wings - You Don't Have To
Say You Love Me - 1-2-3

**ALL WOMAN
VOLUME 3 PVG/CD 9187A**

Almaz - Big Spender - Crazy For You
Fame - From A Distance - My Baby Just
Cares For Me - My Funny Valentine
The Power Of Love - Promise Me
Respect - Take My Breath Away
Total Eclipse Of The Heart

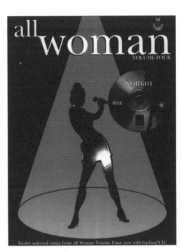

**ALL WOMAN
VOLUME 4 PVG/CD 9255A**

Baby Love - Diamonds Are Forever -
Evergreen - For Your Eyes Only - I Will
Survive - If I Could Turn Back Time - I'll
Be There - Rainy Night In Georgia - Send
In The Clowns - Smooth Operator - Sweet
Love - Touch Me In The Morning

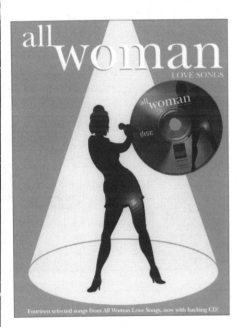

**ALL WOMAN
LOVE SONGS PVG/CD 7502A**

All At Once – Anything For You –
Because You Love Me – Crazy For You –
Didn't We Almost Have It All – The
Greatest Love Of All – Here We Are –
Hero – How Do I Live – I'll Never Love
This Way Again – Saving All My Love For
You – Think Twice – The Wind Beneath
My Wings – Without You

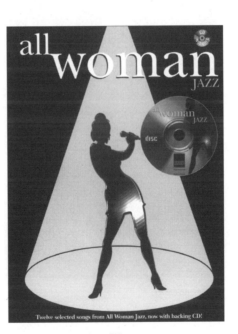

**ALL WOMAN
JAZZ PVG/CD 9500A**

Bewitched – Dream A Little Dream Of Me
A Foggy Day – The Girl From Ipanema
I'm In The Mood For Love – In The
Mood – It Don't Mean A Thing (If It Ain't
Got That Swing) – Misty
Nice Work If You Can Get It – On Green
Dolphin Street – 'Round Midnight
Where Or When

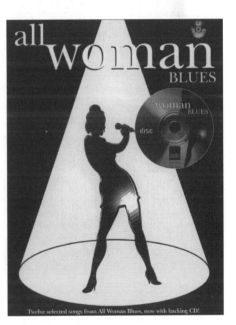

**ALL WOMAN
BLUES PVG/CD 9550A**

The Birth Of The Blues - Come Rain Or
Come Shine - Embraceable You -
Georgia On My Mind - Knock On Wood
Mood Indigo - Night And Day - Rescue Me
Someone To Watch Over Me
Stormy Weather
Take Another Little Piece Of My Heart
What Is This Thing Called Love

Available from all good music shops

YOU'RE THE VOICE

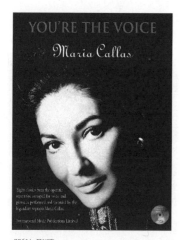

8861A PV/CD

Casta Diva from Norma - Vissi D'arte
from Tosca - Un Bel Di Vedremo from
Madam Butterfly - Addio, Del Passato
from La Traviata - J'ai Perdu Mon
Eurydice from Orphee Et Eurydice - Les
Tringles Des Sistres Tintaient from
Carmen - Porgi Amor from Le Nozze Di
Figaro - Ave Maria from Otello

8860A PVG/CD

Delilah - Green Green Grass Of Home -
Help Yourself - I'll Never Fall In Love
Again - It's Not Unusual - Mama Told Me
Not To Come - Sexbomb Thunderball -
What's New Pussycat - You Can Leave
Your Hat On

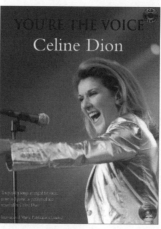

9297A PVG/CD

Beauty And The Beast - Because You
Loved Me - Falling Into You - The First
Time Ever I Saw Your Face - It's All
Coming Back To Me Now - Misled - My
Heart Will Go On - The Power Of Love -
Think Twice - When I Fall In Love

9349A PVG/CD

Chain Of Fools - A Deeper Love
Do Right Woman, Do Right Man - I Knew
You Were Waiting (For Me) - I Never
Loved A Man (The Way I Loved You)
I Say A Little Prayer - Respect - Think
Who's Zooming Who - (You Make Me
Feel Like) A Natural Woman

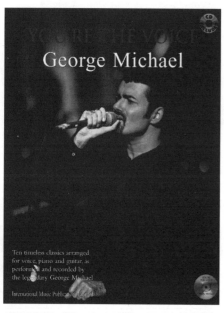

9007A PVG/CD

Careless Whisper - A Different Corner
Faith - Father Figure - Freedom '90
I'm Your Man - I Knew You Were Waiting
(For Me) - Jesus To A Child
Older - Outside

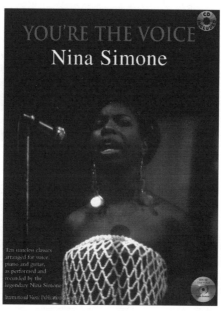

9606A PVG/CD

Don't Let Me Be Misunderstood -
Feeling Good - I Loves You Porgy - I Put A
Spell On You - Love Me Or Leave Me -
Mood Indigo - My Baby Just Cares For Me
Ne Me Quitte Pas (If You Go Away) -
Nobody Knows You When You're Down
And Out - Take Me To The Water

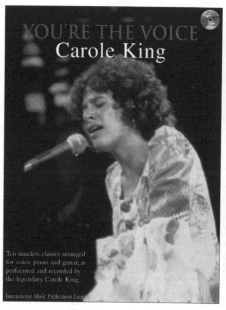

9700A PVG/CD

Beautiful - Crying In The Rain -
I Feel The Earth Move - It's Too Late -
(You Make Me Feel Like) A Natural Woman
So Far Away - Way Over Yonder – Where
You Lead - Will You Love Me Tomorrow
You've Got A Friend

The outstanding vocal series from IMP

CD contains full backings for each song,
professionally arranged to recreate the sounds of the original recording